Process Improvement at the North Pole
With ERNIE the Elf

Jay Poole

Process Improvement at the North Pole

TABLE OF CONTENTS

Introduction	4
Meeting ERNIE the Elf	6
Meeting Santa Claus	18
Santa's Workshop	30
Other North Pole Projects	46
Takeaways	60
Prologue	63

Process Improvement at the North Pole

This book is dedicated to my wife and children

never stop believing.

Process Improvement at the North Pole

Introduction

This story is based on the idea that in order for lean methodologies and process improvements to be successful there has to be a method to remain organized and focused on the task at hand. This book is based on a new higher level overview of what activities should be included in any improvement project. If one takes time to own their improvements, the likelihood of success will be much higher.

Begin with the acknowledgement that each improvement methodology a practitioner utilizes has a sound strategy and should be used based on the specific improvement need. The following is a story about a methodology that takes an approach of identifying a need, working through each step, and continuing the improvement process in future improvement activities. This type of improvement takes the standard bell curve and turns it into

Process Improvement at the North Pole

an "S"- like improvement curve. Utilizing this type of process provides for improvement activities to continue long after the first improvement project is complete.

Examples of improvement strategies one could employ to complete improvement projects are: DMAIC, 5S, Lean, Kaizan, and Kanban. Each of these improvement tools has its own dynamic that provides for one to be successful whether the project focuses on process improvements or reorganizing an area in their organization.

It is the belief that messages of this book are key to the success of ALL improvement projects.

Process Improvement at the North Pole

Meeting ERNIE the Elf

Late one evening I was at my workstation, attempting to solve a problem with one of my projects. While I had been working on this project for a long time, I felt like I was getting nowhere. Every move I made was seen with some progress, but then something would happen and there would be some backsliding, forcing me to rethink the changes I had made and reevaluate each aspect of the change to identify what didn't work. Because of this rework I was starting to miss project milestones, beginning to get frustrated, and second guessing my ability to successfully complete the project.

My project seemed like a fairly straight forward one of re-organizing a production line to maximize efficiencies and minimize defects. This production line has been in operation for thirty years and has been reliable in producing my company's product, but over time the wear and continuous use has resulted in reduced efficiency and more

Process Improvement at the North Pole

product defects. Technology has advanced. So I needed to also include updates where warranted. My manager also asked me to evaluate the work area to identify opportunities for waste reduction and to improve the speed that the product moves through the production line. On top of this, the deadline to have this project completed was rapidly approaching with my manager asking more questions about project status and timeline for completion.

After spending two months evaluating and implementing changes, I felt like I was making progress on improving efficiencies and reducing defects by modernizing obsolete equipment. This progress was made through:

- Reviewing Control Charts

    A method of tracking process performance is used through capturing points of data taken at different parts of the process over time. This provides

Process Improvement at the North Pole

opportunities to identify and address unnecessary variation in the process.

- Developing Spaghetti Diagrams

This is a map of the current workflow state. An example of a spaghetti diagram could be when someone goes to a new grocery store and has to figure out where each item is located. If that person makes a map of how they went it would most likely look like they not only made laps around the store multiple times, but would also show unnecessary movement. Prior to my next visit to this store, I can use this map to remove the extra steps and go straight to the closest item and then work my way from one side of the store to another, minimizing the need to backtrack, walking the same aisle multiple times.

Process Improvement at the North Pole

- Identifying Bottlenecks

    Bottlenecks happen at various stages throughout a process and can be identified by material beginning to back up, making the downstream parts of the process wait to get material. A strategy one can use to address bottlenecks is to level load the process, i.e. establishing a "tempo" for the process to follow. This strategy also aids in decreased waiting time and reduces the work in process inventory.

- Evaluating Wear of Equipment

    This step is addressed by having a preventative maintenance schedule and sticking to it. Depending on demand and available equipment down time, the latter may be hard to do, but developing a schedule of when preventative maintenance is to be performed on each piece of equipment provides for an operating plan to be established.

Process Improvement at the North Pole

From this research, an implementation plan consisting of equipment updates, process flow reorganization, and modified work in process inventory rhythm was developed. In the beginning these modifications showed improvements. Unfortunately, after all these changes, there was at least one unaccounted for variable that was being elusive. Identifying this variable was beginning to cause problems with production line performance.

While deep in thought evaluating different alternatives to identify the unknown variable I heard a loud noise in the hallway outside my work area. Curious, I got up and began walking to the door leading to the hallway. When I opened it, there was a man standing there I had never seen before. This man was dressed differently than I had ever seen anyone dress at work before. He had a pointy hat with no bill, colorful clothes and pointy shoes. Did I miss the office Christmas party?

Process Improvement at the North Pole

Seeing the confusion on my face the man said "Hello, my name is ERNIE."

I was quick to say "Hello" and followed with "Nice to meet you. Did you hear the noise that sounded like a lot of boxes crashing to the floor?"

ERNIE said "Yes, that noise was from me getting onto this floor. The noise was louder than I expected." He then asked if I wanted to see why the noise was so loud. Curiously I said "Sure", not expecting to see much of anything when we walked through the door. At this point, we began to walk to the next door in the hallway, leading to the elevator foyer.

As we walked through the door there was a bright light. The next thing I knew I was in a room I had never seen before. The room contained chairs, tables and refreshments - sort of like a nice lounge area.

Process Improvement at the North Pole

Completely taken off guard of what was going on, I asked ERNIE "Where are we?" ERNIE first gave me a cup of hot chocolate containing marshmallows, and then said, "I know it will be hard to believe, but you are now in Santa's Workshop."

Looking around another time, I noticed the room appeared to be decorated with things like candy canes and garlands around the doorways. I then thought, out of all the places I could arrive at the North Pole, the breakroom wasn't one of them.

I then started to feel like this was a dream and began trying to wake myself up, first by slapping my face and then pinching my right arm. Confused with what he was seeing me do, ERNIE asked "Is there something wrong?"

I responded by saying "This has to be a dream; it can't be happening." ERNIE reassured me this wasn't a

Process Improvement at the North Pole

dream and there was a reason for what was happening. I then asked him to explain.

ERNIE began by saying "I am Santa's Head Elf. One responsibility of being the Head Elf is to find someone every year who can benefit from learning and seeing how elves accomplish tasks and work through unknown situations in Santa's workshop."

I then asked "Why me?"

ERNIE said, "There are many reasons for you being chosen, but the main reason was that you still believe in Christmas and all the good things it stands for."

Continuing, ERNIE said, "I have been watching, seeing how you have been having such a hard time with your project, and felt like it was time for you to come. While your time here will be brief, you are going to see parts of the workshop that may help with getting your project moving forward."

Process Improvement at the North Pole

Given I was at my wits end with where I was with this project I said, "THAT'S GREAT! Where do we begin?"

ERNIE, seeing my eagerness, said "Ok, we are going to first start by giving you time to speak with the man in charge." I immediately said "WHAT did you just say; I am going to see Santa Claus?"

ERNIE responded by a simple "yep" as he began walking towards the door leaving the room.

Following him with excitement, we walked for what seemed like a long time. While walking I kept asking him different questions about what life was like at the North Pole, like what they did in their free time. ERNIE explained that life up there is very busy, but rewarding. Regarding free time, each elf uses their free time differently, so he could only speak for himself. Normally, when not working in the shop, ERNIE likes to tinker on small engines and teach younger elves how to fix engines. ERNIE explained we were

Process Improvement at the North Pole

going to take a quick tour of one part of the toy shop and then eat.

Walking into the toy shop there are multiple production lines running. Elves were moving in different directions performing a variety of tasks on one production line to another. While looking around I see what looks like five individual work areas, work cells. The toys were being made without a lot of wait time between stages of the workflow process. The more I looked it appeared there was a sort of rhythm the elves were using that looked like each elf knew what the other elves were going to do at any particular time.

After looking around for a few minutes ERNIE said, "I'm hungry; let's go get something to eat." So we walked out the door and headed to get a bite to eat at an adjoining building.

Process Improvement at the North Pole

While eating, ERNIE started telling me about what was going to happen next. He began by apologizing that I had not met Santa yet, but this is how the big man likes to start these trips. ERNIE went on to say "Santa likes to wait until you have had a moment to let the fact you are at the North Pole sink in and to get a bite to eat prior to meeting with him."

I said, "Thanks for the heads up, and I appreciate this opportunity. It's hard for me to contain myself."

ERNIE said "This is normal and it won't take long to get focused on why you are here."

While we were finishing eating, ERNIE asked if there was anything else I needed to know before meeting with Santa. I said "no," so we got up and put our dishes away and began to head towards Santa's location.

While walking ERNIE gave me a couple of tips to help me during my meeting with Santa. He said, "Santa will

Process Improvement at the North Pole

take time to fully explain answers to your questions. Refrain from interrupting him. While telling a story he takes time to explain all aspects of it. You will quickly come to find there is a lot of information in his stories that you may be able to use down the road.

Process Improvement at the North Pole

Meeting Santa Claus

It was a long walk to get to Santa's location. While walking , I saw elves painting buildings, and working on the general upkeep of the different buildings we were passing, again in a rhythm appearing to be similar to the one I saw when observing the production line. Ahead of us was a building that looked no different from the others; it had a mixture of brick and wood on the front, with the brick looking red and the wood white. Also, there are green shutters next to the windows. It was a single story building with a sign above the door that says "Claus Inc." As we got to it, ERNIE had me knock on the door. After a few moments the door opened, and there standing before me was the ONE AND ONLY SANTA CLAUS!!!!! He looked just like a picture I saw years ago with his white hair and beard, wearing red pants, white shirt and black boots.

Process Improvement at the North Pole

Santa said, "Hello, you must be the one working on the improvement project ERNIE has been telling me about. I have been waiting to see you and hope you get something out of your trip here. Before we get started, would you mind if I speak with ERNIE for a minute?"

With no hesitation I said "I appreciate this chance and don't mind waiting."

Standing just inside the door Santa had welcomed us through and while I was trying to take everything in, Santa and ERNIE had a brief discussion about the morning and how Operations was going. I vaguely overheard Santa tell ERNIE that the toy train production line was having some problems. It seemed that the wheels were not exactly the same size as they were coming off the line. There had to be something wrong with the molds being used, and he had the Double E's (Engineer Elves) looking into it. ERNIE told

Process Improvement at the North Pole

Santa he would head right over there and support the ongoing trouble-shooting efforts. Santa thanked him.

As he was walking away, ERNIE said, "Good luck! I hope you both enjoy and get a lot out of today."

After ERNIE was gone, Santa started by saying, "Hello, welcome to the North Pole."

I said "Thanks, I could never have dreamed something like this would happen in my whole life."

Santa said "I understand, and because of this being our first meeting, we will start slowly. We can begin with how I got started, including how my operations has evolved over the centuries."

Santa then invited me in his office. I accepted his invitation and start walking down the hallway, following him. After passing a few doors, Santa turned left into a room toward the end of the hallway. After walking in, he sat down in an oversized red arm chair that looked like it had extra

Process Improvement at the North Pole

padding. He told me to sit in a similar arm chair located close to his. . As I looked around, the room was well lit, with a fire place and a green and red square area rug. It also had many pictures of Santa with different people hanging on the wall.

As I sit down, Santa looked at the clock and said, "We better get started."

Santa picked up an itinerary of the plan ERNIE had laid out for my trip. He said, "We are going to discuss how I got started and then begin discussing why you are here and how this visit can help with your current project."

He continued by saying "My goal in telling you my history is so that you will have the right frame of reference of what went into building this workshop."

Santa Tells His History

Santa began, "Just over seventeen hundred years ago, before I became Saint Nick, I spent my time working with children and young adults in a small town in Turkey.

Process Improvement at the North Pole

You see, I have always enjoyed seeing the smiles on children's faces when they get something they really want. Over time, I began leaving the children small toys I would make in my house. As time went by, there were more and more children to whom I was able to provide happiness with small gestures of love through the toys I made. If you want to find more information about my early years, the internet has many stories about how I started my operations."

Santa continued, "As demand for my toys grew, I began developing a system that aided me in providing children the toys they desired. This system started by me getting out and walking around parks and public areas to listen to what children were saying about what toys they most desired. Based on that information, I developed a schedule on what and how many toys I would make. Unexpectedly, after showing my love and guidance, I was granted Sainthood and became immortal. Having the ability to continue focusing on giving to children, the area and

Process Improvement at the North Pole

number of children grew rapidly. Even with continuous growth over the next fifteen hundred years, I was able to maintain a level of production that met demand. I grew little by little and was fortunate to find others who shared this joy and desire to make children happy. As you know, these were the elves. They really came along at a time when I was starting to get behind and having to sacrifice the time I needed to be out listening to what children wanted and instead having to spend more time in the workshop making toys. Over the years, not being able to get out and research what the children wanted started causing problems because I began to accumulate toys I had made too many of due to my not being informed about the number I should produce. Once the elves came in the picture. I was free to get back to getting out and performing my research on what type and number of toys children wanted. Over time, I was able to slowly reduce the excess inventory because there was always some child that still wanted the toys I had made too many of. This

Process Improvement at the North Pole

system worked well until families began to move to distant areas, leading to children believing in me being located on multiple continents."

"In the eighteenth century, I realized there was no way I was going to be able to continue making and distributing toys to all the children who believed in me if I stayed where I was. So, after thinking about all the different towns and cities I was now traveling to I decided to move my operations to a location more centralized to the whole world, and that led us to the North Pole. While being centrally located to the majority of the children who believed in me, from here I could keep my Operations and all its magic hidden from the rest of the world, while also being able to expand my Operations to what it is today."

"'Once my Operations were established I realized I was going to have a hard time staying current with children's wishes. Because of this, I started recruiting people from the

Process Improvement at the North Pole

cities and towns who would be willing to go out, meet children, listen to what they wanted, and then report that information back to me. This was two hundred years before email and cell phones, so I had to devise a communication plan that began with a lag time of two weeks. Also, at this point my reindeer were still in training, so there was no way I could use them to help minimize this excess time. Through the development of centralized routes and handoff points, we were able to reduce the time being wasted transporting information to four days."

"'About a hundred years after the move, I began to see that I was starting to have two problems. Both were centered on how I moved and grew the operation in a rapid manner to keep up with demand. This constant need for production put a lot of stress on both the Operations elves and machines. In addition to this, with the extended distance away from cities and towns, I was getting more and more disconnected with the children. This turned out to be a big

Process Improvement at the North Pole

problem right around the turn of the twentieth century. My inventories began to increase like they did when I was first getting started due to children's wishes being made for toys other than the ones my teams were producing. Fortunately, there were new improvement activities beginning to take shape and I found a way to learn and implement some new strategies."

Santa paused for a moment and said, "I know you are excited and ready to see more, but bear with me a little longer so you can have a complete picture of how the shop was developed. This is the first part of the lesson I am telling you, continue to pay attention to ensure you get the appropriate amount of background prior to our proceeding forward."

Santa continued, "Around the beginning of the twentieth century the industrial revolution was well underway and innovative thinkers were beginning to emerge.

Process Improvement at the North Pole

People were beginning to construct and use strategies incorporating mass production and manufacturing lines that could produce a part the same way consistently. These ideas continued to be developed throughout this time, and fortunately for me the ones developing them were open to sharing so others could also learn. During this time, I disguised some of my elves as people and sent them to these factories to learn. Without the knowledge these people provided, I would still be struggling to meet demand, while also missing the mark when it came to the type of products and quality the operation lines needed to produce. When we go out, you will see these strategies in practice today."

A couple of these improvements were captured from Henry Ford's ideas of mass production, while also incorporating Toyota's strategies of mass customization. If you have been through any type of improvement training - ERNIE said you have been through Lean and Six Sigma training - you have a base knowledge of what these pioneers

Process Improvement at the North Pole

were able to accomplish. From one saying he was only going to produce black cars to another identifying ways to mass customize, strategies for improving efficiency and reliability continue to be made.

"'Now that you have been given an overview of how I got started and what some of the drivers were that have made the shop what it is today, let's get into the reason I brought you here. First, I believe for continuous improvement to work, there must be a strong learning culture. What you are going to see while here will be diverse and ERNIE will be as detailed as possible to ensure you have the entire picture. We are going to start by looking at a project which is centered on a process flow that involves how products move through one Operation from start to finish. This process is one that has been around for a long time and has been a reliable producer. However, recently something is off, and I want you to see how my elves address problems."

Process Improvement at the North Pole

"While accompanying us on this project, you will have ERNIE as your immediate contact for any of the area elves to answer questions. Because our schedule is tight in getting toys out, we have a short period of time to identify the root of problems, implement any adjustments or changes and develop a plan to maintain. If you don't have any questions, let's get started. Santa then got up, opened the door and we walked out."

Process Improvement at the North Pole

Santa's Workshop

While walking from Santa's office to the building containing the process, I started to develop initial questions I was going to ask ERNIE and the elves about the process. I felt that by trying to get as much detail about their process and how problems are solved, I might be able to use that information when I went home to aid in solving my project problems. My first line of questions was going to be focused on finding out how they got baseline information such as: the amount of toys coming through the line each day, the specific types of variation his elves were seeing, how long the problem had existed, and where elves got the guidance regarding what equipment and production line specifics should be. While there were a lot of questions still running through my mind, we made it to the building and there was ERNIE waiting inside the door.

Process Improvement at the North Pole

Santa said "When we started this morning you saw how I sent ERNIE to the area having problems, right? By sending ERNIE, I ensure that the tools we have put in place here are applied consistently. What ERNIE does is to act as a guide. Specifically, he helps in keeping teams focused on addressing the problem. We found there are times a problem can seem to get a lot bigger when one digs deeper into the issues. When this happens there is a chance to do one of two things: remain focused on the initial problem and address the problems that have arisen from it, or have the elves try to address all the problems. Choosing the second option will lead to the end result never getting fixed. Having a pre-established method to address problems has provided a better foundation to be less reactive and more proactive when they come about. Normally I am not in the process area on a frequent basis. I feel the teams are fully capable of running the process. However, every once in a while I come and

Process Improvement at the North Pole

observe elves in action. Since you are here, I am going to hang around and observe how everything is going."

While talking, Santa was looking at some reports and reviewing different graphs located just inside the door at what appeared to be a stand-up workstation. After a minute he told me he was looking to see if there has been a decline in performance of the process ERNIE. After a couple of minutes, while pointing at one of the charts, he looked at me and said he could see where some of the tolerances on one part of the process had started to show excessive variation. He then proceeded to show me a run chart that had a line going up and down between two lines, upper and lower limits (process variation). He said, "See how over here on the left of the chart the variation stays closer to the middle? Now look at how the variation starts to get closer and closer to the upper and lower lines". Santa continued, "Initially, this makes me want to look at some of the molding parts to see if any of them may have become worn". After he had reviewed

Process Improvement at the North Pole

all the reports he looked at me and said, "I start by looking into why a process is behaving a certain way. I like to first look at this type of information so that I have a better idea of where the problem may be located. This way, when I begin looking at the production line, I am better able to rule out potential problem areas as I evaluate potential causes. Now that I have taken a step back and reviewed process performance information, I am now able to see what is being done".

During this time, ERNIE had been waiting for Santa to finish looking at the charts. When finished we went with ERNIE to observe what was going on. While walking ERNIE started to provide Santa a status update.

ERNIE provided a brief summary of actions being taken, finishing by saying, "I believe the work cell team has found the problem and are working towards a solution".

Process Improvement at the North Pole

Speaking to ERNIE, while also looking at me Santa said, "ERNIE, tell him about the process we use when working through problems. Santa then left the conversation and began walking around the process, observing elf activity.

ERNIE started by saying, "Over the centuries we have been developing and refining our process of looking into potential problems and identifying areas for improvement, ensuring appropriate avenues are used to address them." He went on to say, "While it may sound a little corny, the elves and I have structured this activity around the letters of my name E-R-N-I-E. By doing this, an easy to remember framework for process improvement has been put in place providing for a more consistent and reliable result."

ERNIE continued "The great thing about process improvement is there are many different methods one can use to ensure a robust solution is developed and implemented. I

Process Improvement at the North Pole

like to say these are my tools I have in my performance improvement toolbox. These different methods we have evaluated over the years are all good and, if used correctly, will get you to a positive solution. I will go into some of those different methods and how we incorporated them into this model a little later. First, to better make our improvement process hit home and easier to remember, the elves and I wanted to make this process as personal as possible."

ERNIE then began to explain this improvement analysis method by telling me what each letter of his name meant. He then gave me a brief explanation of the meaning behind each of them.

Name:

E – Evaluate,

R – Rank,

N – Navigate,

Process Improvement at the North Pole

I – Implement,

E – Evaluate

Meaning:

Evaluate

ERNIE said, "No matter what the problem or opportunity for improvement is, Evaluate is going to be the first action. Whether you are having an equipment issue, or working to improve a process, evaluating all sides by identifying the depth of the problem and developing a list of actions needing to take place should happen first."

When evaluating, we ask questions like:

- How has the equipment or process been trending?

- Could this be a recurring issue?

- Does the problem present itself in cycles? If so, what is the frequency?

Process Improvement at the North Pole

- How has the problem been fixed in the past?
- Are there areas needing improvement?

Beginning here facilitates the development of a foundation for making decisions on where to start and what will be required to properly address the problem. A well thought out understanding of what needs to happen will begin to develop. The more information which is gathered, along with reviews of past attempts to correct the issue, are good starting points for evaluating and determining the depth of the problem.

Rank

Once a list has been generated of possible solutions, the order in which they are implemented needs to be determined. By taking the time to set an order to when these fixes are to be implemented, actions being taken seem to be more proactive than reactive. This means that we remain deliberate, focusing on the issue at hand, and not going in

Process Improvement at the North Pole

different directions while allowing the scope of the problem to snowball into something we are not able to manage. Developing the ranking order is pretty straight forward, what needs to be done now to get the equipment/process operating again, along with what improvements can be implemented to make it more efficient? Based on this, it will be easier to develop the order of how the solution will be implemented.

Over the past, depending on the depth and scope of the problem, there were times when this step took an extended period of time to get items ranked due to personal feelings and desires to have the list ranked a certain way. This would lead to problems with how the issue was fixed and led to unnecessary added work due to the ranked list not being set up in a manner that provided for the most robust solution. To aid in preventing this from occurring and having a reliable ranked list, we stop and take time to review the goal we developed in the Evaluate stage. This refocusing activity aids with ensuring the list is ranked accordingly and

Process Improvement at the North Pole

the scope of the project remains consistent without unnecessary items being added.

Navigate

This is the part of the process where the top items ranked are further explored to ensure there is a well-rounded and sound implementation. Such items to be considered during this part of the process are:

- How in-depth is the fix, and will the machine need to be down for an extended period of time?

- How immediate is the need? Can the problem be temporarily fixed and allow us to get to a better stopping point?

- If there are new or replacement parts, how long will it take to get them ready to be installed?

Process Improvement at the North Pole

- Will there be any potential unintended consequences during implementation i.e., what other areas may be impacted?

- Can we pilot or test any of the ranked items prior to fully implementing?

From developing answers to these questions, we create a schedule for implementing improvements and can forecast impacts to production schedules and when the project is to be completed.

Implement

Following a well-rounded evaluation of the top ranked items, next is to take these items, using strategies and schedules developed in the Navigate stage, and implement them into the process. During this stage, area elves remain involved ensuring the transition is seamless. While there are many different variables, both known and unknown, which come into play during this stage, it is again important to

Process Improvement at the North Pole

remain focused on the goal and work through them on an individual basis. At times, developing a standardized list to address these known variables can be beneficial. However, each one needs to be taken on an individual basis, ensuring unintended consequences are minimized. Remaining vigilant during this process is key to ensuring a successful project completion.

One of the problems we have encountered at this stage is when there is a need for an extended period of time for items on the schedule to be completed. When this occurs, there are opportunities for the schedule and item due dates begin to slip, which leads to delays on project completion. To prevent excessive amount of schedule slippage, frequent schedule reviews need to occur. During this review a discussion on each item and reliability to meet due dates is held.

Process Improvement at the North Pole

Evaluate

Based on the belief that there will always be areas for improvement, one cannot just stop once the project is complete. This stage is focused on ensuring that changes made are maintained and potential unintended consequences are addressed when they arise. When the project has been fully implemented and schedule completed, the process needs to be monitored to ensure it doesn't return to the condition it was in prior to the project being started. Frequency of this evaluation will be based on how significant the change was and how likely is it for the process to return to the previous state. One of the main factors to consider during this stage is the amount of human interaction. Based on the level of human interaction needed to successfully complete the task at hand, the potential for human variability exists. Additionally, receiving updates from elves running the production line ensures that implemented changes are made, not only to benefit the effectiveness and efficiency of

Process Improvement at the North Pole

the production line, but also to benefit elves who interact with it as well.

After explaining this improvement analysis process to me, ERNIE returned to explaining what was going on with the problem at hand. First he said, "When the elves recognized problems with parts coming off the press section, and transitioning to the assembly section was not coming together as intended, they stopped the section of the process that was producing poor product. Do you see that press over there?" ERNIE asked while pointing to a big piece of equipment that looked like a big stamping machine.

Continuing with his explanation, "If we get a little closer you can see it is a molding machine making train wheels. There is also a template the machine lines up with which ensures that each part is made the same every time." Continuing ERNIE said, "What was happening was, when the wheels were coming off the press, the next stage in the

Process Improvement at the North Pole

process line identified the issue of wheels not being formed according to specifications. This was done before we produced any additional defective parts. We adopted this immediate problem identification process from Toyota's production management system, turning the line into a visual factory. There is a quality check where, when a defect shows itself, production line elves can easily see it due to the system being automated. Elves spend the majority of their time focusing on the product moving through the process rather than attempting to fix the production line while still running. I will go into how the work cells are designed and how material goes through the process at another time." he said, acknowledging he was getting ready to start explaining another strategy the elves use to manufacture trains.

ERNIE continued, "Following a review of the process, elves determined a die had become worn out. After it was replaced the process was restarted and wheels were again in alignment within process specifications".

Process Improvement at the North Pole

I continued to look at what the elves were doing, and it appeared that, while the process had resumed, the head area elf was still writing and speaking with elves. I asked, "What is going on?"

ERNIE said, "Now that the problem has been addressed and run, the head area elf reviews all that was done, including what led to the problem occurring, and then determines what opportunities exist to aid in preventing this problem from occurring in the future.

I said, "So he is looking at the frequency of die change out and whether it needs to be changed more often. Additionally, the head elf is looking into how fast the problem was caught/resolved to improve on the problem identification and resolution in the future."

Process Improvement at the North Pole

Other North Pole Projects

After seeing how elves responded to the train production line problem, I wanted to hear more about other problems they have addressed which might help me in working through my current project problem.

Seeing my excitement ERNIE said, "We can continue this discussion over a cup of hot chocolate, sitting in a location better suited for us to talk." With that we left the workshop area and went back to the building where the breakroom I first entered the North Pole was located.

After getting settled into a nice padded chair next to the fire, ERNIE and I continued our discussion. ERNIE sat in the chair close to me and began by saying "I am sure you and Santa covered a lot this morning. While talking, Santa always covers how the workshop grew over the years, leading up to how big it has become. One area of this growth we had to work on was how our parts warehouse was

Process Improvement at the North Pole

maintained. Without going back over what Santa told you, the main issue we ran into when the big growth occurred was how we were unable to keep everything organized, which led to the overall warehouse operation becoming unorganized and making it hard to retrieve and distribute items."

I then said, "I am sure that caused a lot of problems with getting items in and out in a timely manner."

ERNIE continued, "Yes we were having a hard time with staying on time with production schedules. Using the method we had developed, E-R-N-I-E, we went to work to improve the situation. First, we gathered as much information about the Parts warehouse from area elves. This information included the layout, where items were being stored, and how often each item was being used/retrieved. We even drew a map of how elves went to get items. Another word for this workflow map is a spaghetti diagram. Following this information gathering and speaking with area

Process Improvement at the North Pole

elves, we sat down and looked at the warehouse as a whole and at all the individual parts/processes that make it up. From this session, which we call EVALUATE, we began separating all the items into groups and reviewing how elves were retrieving them.

ERNIE continued, "Following this, we began to RANK what items were most important for us to address now and what would be taken care of later. Some areas we identified to work on now were item shelving location, and flow of how elves retrieved the parts."

Continuing, ERNIE said, "At the North Pole we like to keep everything as simple as possible. To aid with making sure the right part is in the right location, the system we developed involves labeling the shelves and parts: NAVIGATE. First we labeled all part locations on shelves throughout the warehouse. Then, when parts arrived, we made sure there was a label placed on them which

Process Improvement at the North Pole

corresponded to the appropriate shelve. From there, elves worked to develop a flow of getting the parts in the correct location. Basing decisions on the previously developed spaghetti diagram, elves took miles off their activities through having a plan on how and when shelves were stocked and items retrieved throughout the day: IMPLEMENT.

My question to ERNIE was how he sustained the changes after they were fully implemented. ERNIE said, "When explaining this project to you, I gave a very high-level explanation. In the past, one area we found that was always needed monitoring was that, following project completion, there would always be some kind of slippage back to the previous way tasks were being completed. Because of this, the elves developed a strategy and checklist to monitor the area where changes were made. Keeping area elves involved throughout the improvement process is key with ensuring these changes are in line with what needs to be

Process Improvement at the North Pole

done and are standardized." ERNIE went on to say this method has not only provided for progress to be maintained, but has allowed for additional improvement activities to be identified and implemented, EVALUATE.

After finishing our conversation on the parts warehouse, I was still interested in learning more. While it was getting late, I asked ERNIE if he would be willing to share one more story.

ERNIE said he would and began by saying "This next project was a big part of the lifeline of the North Pole and without it we would not be able to get all the toys made and delivered to the right child every year." ERNIE continued, "The problem was how children's files were not being maintained in a central location. Basically there was no formal method for keeping wishes in line with gifts as they were being made. This caused problems by adding a lot of time toward the end of the year when elves were trying to

Process Improvement at the North Pole

organize Santa's sleigh. What I am getting ready to tell you is very confidential and could get me in a lot of trouble. Telling you how wishes are recorded and answered is something we keep a tight control over. Because of this, I am not going into specifics in a couple of areas, but I will provide you enough information so that you can get a good idea of how the problem was captured and addressed."

ERNIE then took a moment to get his thoughts together and have another drink of marshmallow filled cocoa.

ERNIE resumed his story by saying, "First, this was not a one elf project. Many elves had to be involved to ensure everything was covered prior to Implementing the solution. Beginning with the Scope, how widely are files dispersed while actively answering the wish? Additionally, we worked on developing a baseline of how files were currently being updated and tracked. On top of this, we drew

Process Improvement at the North Pole

a process map that showed the current state of how files flowed through the North Pole.

ERNIE continued, "While EVALUATING all the documents and flow diagrams, the team was also looking at potential central locations for the files to be located, with only necessary information being sent to identify areas. During this time, we drew a spaghetti diagram. With a goal of having a streamlined workflow with less than one percent defects, the team was aiming pretty high, seeing how there was no formal workflow and more than nine and a half percent defects. Focusing on the current workflow and spaghetti diagram, the team looked at developing a critical path for files by determining what needed to be in each file and how it should be organized. Basing file organization on how the workflow is sequenced provides more standardization while the wish is moving through the granting process. This aids elves by not having to fumble through papers to get what they need when completing their

Process Improvement at the North Pole

tasks. We finally decided the central location for all files would be in Santa's Naughty and Nice work area. This area had extra room and could handle the additional work flowing through it. The more we thought about it, the more we thought that, if we could, we would use Santa's book of wishes; i.e., the center of the process where information flows from and comes back at the end."

ERNIE again said "This information is NOT to be shared with anyone". ERNIE then continued, "Basically, a child makes a wish and asks for something from Santa. The wish is automatically recorded in the book". I commented, "Like how a person puts an item in a basket when they are making an online order and, when they complete the order, notifications are then sent to respective areas for completion?" ERNIE said that was correct and then he continued, "You have to think, this was before the electronic age and internet, so we were basically trying to do this from scratch without anything to look at while developing it."

Process Improvement at the North Pole

I then asked ERNIE, "So let me get this straight. Your process included a magic book that recorded wishes, and elves had to interact with it to update each time a wish was made. When it was complete, ready for Santa to deliver, you also had separate files which were taken around while the wishes were being turned into reality? That seems like a lot of double work, while also creating room for error."

ERNIE responded "Yes, it has been a big headache and we are still working on this project getting all the kinks worked out. There is still unnecessary transportation of both the files and inventory". He continued by saying, "This new workflow continues to be a work in progress for us, and with each year we are making minor adjustments which are showing big gains in accuracy and efficiency over time. I always have to remind myself that patience and perseverance will pay off in the long run as long as I maintain focus on the end target".

Process Improvement at the North Pole

I then asked ERNIE, "So, it sounds like you have not completed this project?" ERNIE reaffirmed "You are right. After RANKING, what was most important to implement was a standardized workflow and improved efficiencies with the route in which wish files are moved throughout the workshop. We reviewed the spaghetti diagram and current workflow to determine what could be implemented to not only to decrease the amount of time it took for the wish to be completed, but also to reduce the amount of time required for rework: NAVIGATE. From this we began to IMPLEMENT items such as the standardized folder, we reorganized workflow so toys not only spent less time going through the process, but also reduced the down time between toys being made on the process line".

ERNIE continued, "We remain in the EVALUATE stage, continuing to identify these areas for improvement and conducting small projects to improve. The biggest part about

Process Improvement at the North Pole

any improvement process is that there will always be areas for improvement".

I responded by saying, "Yes, I agree. It's just like this project I have been working on. I am not only having to take a piece of equipment and modify it to fit the latest requirements for the new part we are going to produce, but with the modification I also have to realign the remaining areas of the process to ensure transitions are seamless between each stage".

The more I thought about it, the sleepier I became. Following the discussion of how children's files were being handled, I began thinking about everything ERNIE and I had covered and what I might be able to…

"Jay!"

…use when I get back to working on my project. I reflected on one reason my project was not going well was

Process Improvement at the North Pole

because I was trying to do it alone, I need to get more people from the work area involved.

"Jay, Jay, can you hear me?"

Just then, my eyes began to open and I asked, "Where am I?"

I then heard the voice of my coworker say "Jay, are you awake? Its 7:30 am, you must have fallen asleep here last night. You need to get freshened up before the rest of the group gets in."

After waking up and looking around the work area, I thought to myself, "If I was asleep, that was the truest dream I ever had. It felt like everything I was doing was real".

While getting up to go to the restroom to freshen up, my coworker asked, "would you like some coffee?"

Knowing I didn't keep a coffee cup at work I said, "No, I do not have a cup." My coworker then said, "what

Process Improvement at the North Pole

about that coffee cup?" Looking at the corner of my desk I saw the cup with a candy cane on the side that ERNIE had given me when we arrived at the North Pole."

Just then, my morning fog went away, everything in the room faded away to the background as I focused on the coffee cup. I began to question whether everything that had happened was real. The more I thought about it, the more I wanted to say "Yes, I did go to the North Pole last night!"

But if I didn't go, I wondered if someone had left their coffee cup on my workstation sometime yesterday and I just didn't notice. I continued thinking about this while walking to the bathroom to get freshened up.

After freshening up and getting back to my workstation, I thought that, whether it was real or not, I was going to look at my project and determine how I could use what ERNIE and I did the night before. First I started reaching out by contacting area workers. While I had spoken

Process Improvement at the North Pole

with them briefly throughout my project, I had not really sat down and discussed what I was trying to do with them while also getting their thoughts on what they thought would work and bouncing my ideas off them to get their input. The more I thought about it that had been one of the biggest mistakes of my project.

The deeper I got into solving my problems with this project, the more confident I felt in making decisions. I went back and used ERNIE's method to complete projects: EVALUATE, RANK, NAVIGATE, IMPLEMENT, and EVALUATE. Breaking each part of my project up and starting with identifying what the goal and scope of my project was helped bring me back on track. Before I knew it, I had completed the equipment modification. I made plans for improving the workflow and established a method for monitoring changes to aid with ensuring that there would be no process backsliding.

Process Improvement at the North Pole

Takeaways

Now that some time has passed since my time with ERNIE, I have reflected and identified two takeaways. One, a person should own the improvement process. The other takeaway was ERNIE's willingness to take me around and show me improvement activities. On top of that, while my time was brief, he spent time discussing other projects, focusing on explaining key aspects and answering my questions to ensure I fully understood.

Owning the improvement process not only takes the person conducting the project, but also must involve the entire organization. When I arrived at the North Pole, I spoke with ERNIE and Santa. I then went on the production floor and observed the interaction between Santa, ERNIE and area elves. This type of strategy was based on the fact that involving everyone provided for a more reliable solution. A secondary benefit was the fact that the more opportunities

Process Improvement at the North Pole

area elves had to be involved in projects, the more likely they were to retain and implement improvement principles and strategies.

Finally, by ERNIE taking time to discuss my project and all the projects he had worked on provided a learning opportunity for both of us. ERNIE was able to get a different perspective on how one handles improvement activities. I on the other hand was provided an opportunity to speak with a person who was well versed with process improvement and able to teach me areas I did not have a lot of experience in. The mentoring relationship we developed during our time has brought about the desire for me to also become a mentor to provide another up and coming improvement professional the chance to learn not only from my successes, but also from my mistakes.

Whether what I did and saw with ERNIE was real or just a dream, I remain committed to believing, no matter how

Process Improvement at the North Pole

big the project or problem, there will always be a solution. It may take time to fully develop and implement, but with a broad knowledge of process improvement strategies along with patience, perseverance and reinforcement the solution will be achieved.

Just as Santa understood he could not complete everything by himself when he began to use elves, we also need to realize we are not on an isolated island with a population of one. Identify and utilize needed resources to assist during tough assignments.

<u>EVERYTHING STARTS WITH BELIEVING</u>

Process Improvement at the North Pole

Prologue

In closing, I believe there needs to be some forward looking commitments to aid with continuous growth and facilitation of lean strategies. I challenge you, the reader, to work on the following:

- First, life is a journey where we never stop learning. Take time to read and discuss books and how they relate to your life with others.
- Second, having education and experience means a lot. No matter what your experience level, I challenge you to find a person and work with them so they can learn from your experiences and you from theirs.

www.ingramcontent.com/pod-product-compliance
Lightning Source LLC
Chambersburg PA
CBHW071431220526
45469CB00004B/1496